On the Bright Side

Andrew Aldred

chipmunkapublishing
the mental health publisher

Andrew Aldred

All rights reserved, no part of this publication may be reproduced by any means, electronic, mechanical photocopying, documentary, film or in any other format without prior written permission of the publisher.

>Published by
>Chipmunkapublishing
>United Kingdom

http://www.chipmunkapublishing.com

Copyright © 2016 Andrew Aldred

ISBN 978-1-78382-293-5

On the Bright Side

Dedication

To Jane

Andrew Aldred

On the Bright Side

Biography

Andrew Aldred has served in the British Army. He has had a psychiatric history dating back some thirty years. He has suffered from depression, anxiety, bipolar, schizophrenia, psychosis and paranoia. He has served time in secure mental hospital and prison. He has been married and is currently divorced. This book was written at the time of his recent divorce. It contains poetry about a wide variety of subjects, and short stories about various topics, including cannibalism, mental illness, rape, sexuality, religion, terrorism, army discipline, and drug abuse. Andrew currently works for the Recovery Academy at Prestwich Hospital.

Andrew Aldred

Emptiness

Now that my wife has gone
Taking all of her family with her
I am left with nothing to do
And no purpose in life
I have been retired from the army
Since I was forty years' old
And I don't know what to do for a living
They gave me a pension
It's a blessing and a curse
I've got money but I don't have to work
They don't give disabled people jobs
I've decorated the house
And sorted everything out inside it
Nobody really wants to know me
And I'll be fifty next year
I've got to go out and find a new life

On the Bright Side

Mother

She has worked as hard as anyone
In this family
To keep us all alive
She taught in schools
For nearly fifty years
She's stuck to my father like glue
And held the family together
She believes in women's rights
But she doesn't believe women should go in pubs
She's been an artist since she retired
She had three children
One of whom she lost
In tragic circumstances
All through my time in prison and hospital
She would answer the phone
And make time to see me
She's not a quitter
And very well meant
And since I've grown older
I've learnt to appreciate her more
I was a difficult child

Andrew Aldred

Culture of Intolerance

There's a culture of intolerance these days
People suffering from road rage
And people with webcams filming them
Everyone wants to come out on top of the heap
The kids know the law from an early age
And they think nothing of accusing the older generation
Of sex crimes and the like
The police spend half their time
Sorting out the worlds' problems
As well as dealing with serious crime
Most people live in a world
They don't quite understand
And can't come to terms with
That makes them intolerant and angry
And a pain in the backside for everyone else

On the Bright Side

Two Generations on

I notice my age when I go into record shops
I don't know half the stuff on the shelves
Particularly if they only sell CD's
I realize I've been a grandfather
And I'm two generations behind
The people that buy records
There's just a handful of classic rock LP's
And a great deal of dance and R'n'B
They don't cater for people like me
In the trendy shops in Manchester
They're all for the students
I have to get my stuff off Amazon
All I can get is re-releases
The originals have long gone
And I'm two generations on

Andrew Aldred

Single Again

I don't have to watch television
When I don't want to
No one is screaming at me
To change my underpants
Or wear deodorant
I can go to sleep on the settee
And stay there all night
I've decorated the house how I want
And got rid of all her feminine traces
Her collection of dolls and soft toys
Went away with her make-up and jewelry
I actually have time to fix the car and do the garden
And cook for myself
I'm free of her at last
And I'm single again

On the Bright Side

The New Age of Comedy

I've taken a bit of time off
To watch comedy on television recently
The comedians are very sharp and witty
And stylish in suits
But very few of them are actually funny
People are laughing in the audience
But I think they only do it because they're supposed to
These comedians are all college boys
From the better universities
You don't get any of the old breed
People like Tommy Cooper and Les Dawson
Although there are still a few stars
That do some good TV shows
Remember Phoenix Nights, Blackadder
Mr. Bean and Coogans's Run
Some of which had me falling out of my chair
Most comedians are doing it
Because its' easier than a proper job
An hour a night
With an audience
Desperate to please you with their laughter
You can get away with being crap
If you look the part

Andrew Aldred

Cast Adrift

There's very few people that want to know me
In this new age of freedom
My wife and her family
Have disappeared off the horizon
My brother visits me every other weekend
Will he get sick of me as well?
Does he come because he wants to?
Or just because he thinks he's doing his disabled brother
A favor by keeping an eye on him?
I've got a friend that comes round
For a cup of tea and a chat
But he's not there a lot of the time
I'm trying to fill my life
With doing day to day chores
Trying to look after myself
Thinking about writing a book of fiction
Trying to gather some detail
And give the ideas I have some structure
I'd better keep a tight grip on myself
The neighbors aren't talking to me
I'm all on my own in this dirty town
And I'm going to have to get on with it

On the Bright Side

My Brother

As a harmonica player he is brilliant
He's a good father
To his only son
He looks after our parents
Where I could not stand
More than a week of their company
He holds the family together
By coming to see me every two weeks
But he has very little life of his own
He's propping everyone else up
But it's at his own expense
He could be out playing the harmonica
Or doing a job
I hope his life doesn't hold him back forever
From doing what he wants to with his career
But he's a good son and a good father
Something I was never destined to be

Andrew Aldred

The Chimney

They came and turned it grey
Two scallywags from God knows where
They smeared mortar all over it
And left it a mess
A good neighbor has volunteered
To sort it out for a reasonable sum
He's cleared the residue off
And re-laid the top two courses of bricks
It will be finished next week
And I will pay the money
That he deserves for the task
And I hope I can forget about the chimney
And all the upset it has caused
For a good long time

On the Bright Side

Dinosaurs of Rock

They've opened up the coffins of the undead
In the morgue of rock music
Everyone's got out of bed
To do a last "Greatest Hits" tour
And relive their glory days
From nineteen seventy-five
It never gets any easier
For the undead rock stars
Performing for the next generation
Of long haired fans in their teens
But they've got to pay
For the new roof on their country house
And the education of their third wife's children
So they do what they can
They're out there on stage tonight
Barely able to stand up through the gig

Andrew Aldred

Opting Out

I could go speed dating in Manchester
Or telephone a local slag
But my heart isn't in it
I couldn't start all over again
I don't want to lose all my money twice
I'm not interested in playing the field
Now that I'm fifty years' old
I'll leave all that to my ex-wife
Good luck to her and everybody else
The rest of the world can get on
I'll be opting out

On the Bright Side

Extra Mileage

I own a battered old Citroen
It's needed a few jobs doing recently
A new headlight
I've yet to get a new exhaust
The timing belt has been replaced
And I've done some spraying and fiber-glassing
On the bodywork myself
To keep it as good as it can be
I can't afford a new car
This one will have to do
And I need the extra mileage

Andrew Aldred

Alone but not Lonely

Someone once said to me
"You're one in a million"
And I realized that
I am also one in those million
There's nothing special about me
I might spend most of my time at home
But there's a world full of people
In Farnworth and Bolton
And further afield in Manchester
I might not have much
But I'm better off than a lot of people
Just like the old song "Streets of London"
There's people worse off everywhere
And London is no different
To anywhere else
I'm alone by choice
I prefer my own company
And there's a world outside my doorstep

On the Bright Side

Good as You

Someone once told me
The word "gay" stands for "good as you"
I would agree with that
I see a lot of credible gay people
Doing all sorts of things in life
What worries me
Is will we ever see the end
Of the sexual revolution
There's a new edition of "Frozen"
On television this year on Christmas Day
I watched the last one
And I don't think we should be selling
Any sort of sexuality to people who can't walk yet
I liked it when "true love's kiss"
Was shared by a boy and a girl
I honestly don't believe gay people need to fight their corner
They are increasingly accepted in society
Is gay going to be the new normal?
It's not up to me but I'll still be heterosexual

Andrew Aldred

Send in the Bombers

There's been a lot of talk recently
About Islamic State and Isis
No one's talking about it any more
Everyone is sick of hearing about
Child soldiers and beheadings
And mass slaughter of women and children
The shootings in Paris
Were the perfect excuse
They took a hundred and thirty lives
And they'll pay for it with thousands
The West will not tolerate
People who still live in the Dark Ages
And want to act out the Crusades again
Syria will be razed to the ground
And totally rebuilt
They're sending in the bombers

On the Bright Side

We Built a Palace

We built a magnificent palace together
A building in its own grounds
Was it a monstrosity to you?
I'll never know
Did it feel like a prison?
Maybe to you that's what it was
We ended up tearing it down
Brick by brick, wall by wall
Now it's a derelict waste ground
I was so proud of what we did
But now there's nothing left
Of my dream I built for you
We built a palace and destroyed it
Eight years is a long time

Andrew Aldred

A Sunny Day

She's been very ill recently
With pneumonia and a chest infection
We're outside the hospital
Having a well-earned cigarette
We want to make a go of it
It's a winter's day
And the sun is shining
Spring is coming
Giving us new hope
She nearly died last night
At least I was there for her
Her mother isn't well
And she needs my help
We have to realise
We are still in love
And we can't shake it off
Even after the events of last year
We've got through winter
She's going to get better
The sun is shining
Giving us new hope

On the Bright Side

Independence

You see them in the city
The independent people
With their fancy sports cars
And their designer gadgets
Parading around
Pretending they got there by themselves
But they still have to work for someone
They still have a boss
And considerable responsibilities
As well as a twenty-year-old stud
For a sexual partner
They're all cock and no balls
Their bubble hasn't burst yet
Nothing has come along to destroy them
They are intact in their own little worlds
They think they're living
But they haven't lived
None of them got there all by themselves
Even a test tube baby
Still had a mother and a father
Somewhere in the past
Show me someone who is totally independent
And I'll show you a liar

Andrew Aldred

The EU Referendum

We would be one vote in twenty-eight
If we voted to stay in the EU
We would be joining forces
With a lot of countries
Who can't manage their economies
Under what the German chancellor hopes
Will be a new united Europe
Europe is our main trading partner
But we also buy a lot of European goods
Would there be a trade embargo?
Would Europe co-operate with us
In matters of border control,
Terrorism and criminal justice?
Would we be better off alone?
Will Scotland leave us for the EU?
There's a lot of questions to be answered
Things nobody can predict
I hope the British public
Has a better idea than I
Of what is best for our country

On the Bright Side

Genital Mutilation

I heard a program about circumcision
On the radio today
They were saying that they should wait
Until children were old enough
To make their own decisions
About whether to get circumcised
I've been old enough to make my own decisions
For a while now
Being fifty years of age
And getting circumcised has never entered my head
Until I heard the radio broadcast today
They are bringing in laws
To protect children's human rights
But only in cases where the child's parents
Dispute the act of mutilation
It's a bit late after three thousand years of it
There is no good reason for it
Just a load of outdated religious claptrap
First we heard about female genital mutilation
Parents and relatives can be guilty of a lot
Genital mutilation is not a solution for anything
Just a corruption of the bodies God gave us
For the sake of some bizarre custom
Or primitive set of ideas
That are no longer relevant in today's world

Andrew Aldred

Cyber Crime

I had my email account compromised today
Someone's spying on me
Or someone is trying to take my identity
I check my bank account
And change my email account password
In the hope it will foil the predator
I give the details to nobody
I can't trust anybody
It may be a simple error of some sort
But this is paranoia city for me
I've had people scam my computer before
Claiming to be selling software
To make my computer run faster
I've even paid money for it
There's very few people who haven't been scammed
In this day and age
I've had to take out indemnities
On my bank account
I've just bought a new computer
And I'm not allowing anyone else to use it
I'm keeping all my details locked away
Out of sight of prying eyes
There's only one safe place for personal details
And that's in my own memory

On the Bright Side

Racism and the Media

We've recently heard Ken Livingstone
And another Labour member of parliament
Talking about Palestine
And mentioning Hitler and Zionism
And revealing some sort of factual evidence
That the Nazis and the Jewish hierarchy
Both wanted the Jewish nation to move
To their ancient homeland in Jerusalem
It's no wonder that after the concentration camps
And the genocide of Jewish people
The remarks of Ken Livingstone
Cause huge offence to Jews
And the Palestinian people
Who live on the Gaza strip
Have been oppressed for years
By the Jewish government
What the world wants is a real solution
Palestinians and Jews living in the same community
Without racial hatred over who really owns the land
Entrenched attitudes and paranoia
Prevent people living in harmony
There comes a time for forgetting the past
And getting on with the future
The comments of misguided politicians
And sensationalist media
Never helped anybody

Andrew Aldred

Con Men

I clocked them as soon as I got to the service station car park
Two heavily built men intent on selling stolen goods
They pulled up in their van and asked me if I wanted to buy a television
I said I didn't and went into the service station to take a piss
When I came out they hassled me again
They got onto some other people and sold two stolen televisions
Then they came back to me and asked me to wind down my window
The salesman asked me to come and look in the back of his van
He knocked down the price by fifty quid and asked me again
The TVs looked properly packaged and legitimate and I was tempted
I said I'd go to the cash machine and get the money he wanted
He loaded one of the TV sets in the back of my car and waited
I came back with the money and the deal was done
When I got home I unpacked the stolen television
And found the flat screen TV in the packaging was damaged beyond repair
I took it to the tip the next day having learned my lesson
People selling stuff at your door or in a public place are never any good

On the Bright Side

The Magic Roundabout

My former wife and I are now living apart
We still love each other
But God bless our two separate houses
And the small amount of time we have to ourselves
Away from the magic roundabout of life
As it carries on spinning out of control
We have to somehow keep the family out of debt
And look after our aging relatives
After a lifetime of mental illness
And substance abuse without any break
It all gets too much at times
We have to give ourselves a rest
From each other and everyone else
One day we'll both fall off
The wheel as it spins
And that will be the end of us
We've sorted out our wills recently
And at least we've got something to leave behind
For the rest of our families
To help them keep going until they too expire
And leave it to their next generation

Andrew Aldred

Lagging Behind

I don't seem to be able to get more work
Nobody will give me any
Everyone else is moving forward
My ex-wife's daughter will pass her degree next year
My ex-wife has given up drinking and smoking
Her nephew is in work
My brother is getting more employment
I've given up drinking but I still smoke
I feel as if my best years are behind me
I wonder what I can do
And whether I am capable of very much else
Apart from filling in for everyone else
With odd jobs and driving
My father's had a heart attack
On top of his recent cancer
My ex-wife's mother has got out of hospital again
And seems to be on top for the time being
I wish I could sit back for awhile
And forget about impending disaster
But life goes on and always will
I'm starting to tire and I'm lagging behind

On the Bright Side

Disabled

It was the mid nineteen nineties. John, Callum, Brendan and Maggie were on an all-day session at a pub in North Manchester. They were an IRA cell due to plant a bomb on a bus between Manchester and Bolton. It was a time between the Manchester bombings and the IRA ceasefire.

They had been drinking cider at a bar in Bolton town-centre that was in much need of refurbishment, as most of the bars in that particular town were at the time. Callum, an ex-Foreign Legionnaire was talking to an ex-soldier from the British Army who seemed to have got washed up at the same pub that day. They had been playing pool and listening to the jukebox, which played a mixture of heavy metal, music from the "Manchester" scene and rave tunes. Everybody was wildly drunk, and Maggie was being accosted by one of the locals, who thought he fancied her, a mistaken idea in her eyes, as she attacked him, fists flailing, to be hauled off and calmed down by John, the leader of the "gang", an older Irishman, and a figure of authority to the rest of them. He paid their rent and he was the "boss".

After sinking some twenty pints of cider that day, because they had all got their dole money, they went back to their flat to continue the party. They invited the ex-soldier to their flat to have a little "fun" with him. He didn't know it, but at the very least he was going to get a good beating.

They got back, having stopped at the off-licence for some two-litre bottles of white lightning cider and some bitter to make "snakebite" with. The taxi driver was paid off and the motley crew disappeared upstairs.

Callum played his rebel songs on the stereo, and the ex-soldier sang along with him to the raucous tunes, glad to have some company and someone to party with, having a lonely existence in a flat of his own, somewhere on the other side of town. They all popped some pills together, and shortly after this it turned nasty. John turned to the ex-soldier and said "I don't like the way you have treated me". The ex-soldier, sensing danger, said, "Give me a minute and

Andrew Aldred

I'll be on my way". As he gathered his belongings together, Maggie started shouting at him, and as Brendan opened the door, John and Maggie kicked at his legs as he staggered downstairs. They got rid of him and closed the door, keeping his leather coat, which was the only thing he had worth having.

They discussed him afterwards. "What an arsehole", said John to Callum. "Thinking he can sing our songs with us. Thinking we're his best mates. We should have given him more than a kicking". "Nah", said Callum, "He was just some fellah wanting a bit of company." "Don't forget what side you're on", said John. "That bastard was still from the British Army". "Anyway, fuck him. He's gone", said Callum. "Tomorrow we're going to blow up a bus", said John. "I'll drink to that", said Brendan from the corner of the room. Glasses were raised, the rest of the booze was drunk, and the four people collapsed in a drunken heap and woke up the next morning with king-size hangovers.

The following morning John received a telephone call from his superiors in Ireland telling him to stand down. They wanted him to wait before planting the bomb to see whether they could come to some agreement with the British government about a ceasefire. John was not happy. "Them bastards Martin McGuinness and Gerry Adams, they've sold us down the river", he said. He resolved to plant the bomb on the number eight bus that afternoon, after talking to the rest of his rebel band. Callum was the only one who remained strangely silent. He was the only one who had any knowledge of explosives, and the one who had built and would arm the device. Brendan and Maggie got on the bus to Manchester with the rucksack the bomb was housed in shortly before midday. They went to Manchester, leaving the bomb on the bus, had a quick pint at a town-centre pub and came back on the train, confident the bomb would go off on the way back to Bolton. They got back to Bolton and turned on the television to hear the news.

They all sat in the flat waiting but there was no major headline. The only major news was that there was going to be an IRA ceasefire. At the end of the news bulletin there

On the Bright Side

was a small piece about an unexploded device found on a bus. John turned on Callum. "Did you set the device correctly and do what I told you to do?", he said. Callum replied, "Some of us believe in a united Ireland. What if Adams and McGuinness can pull it off?". John said, "You bastard. What do you think we're all here for? To plant fucking bombs or just to go on the piss!" Callum said nothing. He stood up and walked towards the door. John said, "I'll give you one chance to walk away from me, the IRA, and everything you've ever known. Just step through that door." Callum said, "I'll take my chance." He walked off into town and never looked back. He registered homeless, got himself somewhere to live, went to college and landed a job in the automobile industry. As for the rest of them, who knows?

Andrew Aldred

Fighting Girls

Marie and Annette sat together on the couch. Maria's daughter, Marissa was on the floor with her boyfriend. They were sat in Maria's living room drinking lager and watching a film on television. The room was in chaos, with empty pizza boxes on the floor, which hadn't seen a hoover in ages. The curtains were stained and dirty and the room stank of smoke, mainly from Maria's cannabis habit, which was beyond a joke. She smoked reefers like most people smoked cigarettes and was psychologically addicted to the substance. There was a picture of a naked woman smoking a huge joint on the wall in front of the fire which said a lot about the occupants of the house.

Maria was a large woman with a face a trucker would have been proud of. She stood six feet tall and was heavily built with tattoos of her boyfriend and her daughter's name on either arm. She had a reputation for violence and drinking in her local town, and that reputation was well-earned. She had beaten many a man up for coming on to her "family" of Annette and her daughter, Marissa. She wore gold-plated rings on her hands, a complete set of them, and they served as knuckle-dusters.

Annette was "the pretty one" of the three girls, and the one that got most attention. She was an exercise and sex junkie and got plenty of both. She was half-Spanish, with blond hair and a swarthy complexion, wearing heavy make-up and having a car, which made her a useful friend for Maria and her daughter.

Marissa and her current boyfriend, a mechanic called Ryan asked if they could borrow the bed. Maria complained, but gave in to her daughter, saying they had both better be out of there by the time Annette and herself got home from the pub. Marissa and Ryan went upstairs to get on with what they had started in front of everyone in the living room. Maria told her daughter to remember contraception existed

On the Bright Side

and that if she got pregnant she would be thrown out of the house.

Maria and Annette got ready to go out in the living room, Annette in a skimpy black dress and high-heels and Maria wearing a white blouse and jeans and a black leather jacket. They went to a local pub not far away, and got drunk, having some banter with the locals, who fancied Annette. They were told by Maria, "Leave her alone, she's my bitch!" The girls played pool and drank a good few more pints of lager. They staggered home, arm in arm at half past twelve to find the house empty. "I wonder where the bastards are?" said Annette to Maria, the bastards being the two women's boyfriends. "They're up to no good in the town-center" replied Maria. "Well, we can do the same here" said her friend. They embraced and kissed, taking their clothes off as their passion for each other grew. "Fuck the bastards!" said Maria to Annette.

"The bastards" were Ronnie and Paul, the two women's boyfriends. Ronnie was a cage-fighter, who generally won more than he lost and was thought of as "good value for money" by the punters. Paul was the other "bastard", a continental trucker who was Maria's boyfriend. He supplied her with cannabis from Holland, along with half the neighborhood. They had a violent relationship that had lasted a lot longer than it should have, nearly ten years to be exact.

Maria and Annette had lesbian sex before Maria went into a deep sleep on the couch whilst her friend made a cup of coffee in an attempt to sober up before she drove home. She valued her driving license

As she drank her coffee there was a knock on the door. It was the "bastards", Ronnie and Paul, drunk and rampant and also pissed off that half the girls in town had turned them down that night knowing they were trouble.

They came in and immediately noticed that Annette was in her underwear and Maria was half-dressed and comatose on the couch. Ronnie said to Annette "You've been up to each other, haven't you?". Annette said nothing and Ronnie and Paul looked at each other and Ronnie said "You don't think that will go without punishment, do you?" He grabbed her by the hair, saying "Scream, and I'll break your neck". The men took her upstairs and raped her. Annette was quite used to rough treatment from Ronnie but this went too far. They took advantage of Annette until they had satisfied themselves and fell asleep in the double bed whilst she got her clothes on and got into her car crying.

Maria slept through everything, and when she woke up the next morning, the men told her they had sex with her friend, on which point she flew into a rage, grabbed a carving knife and threw both the men out of the house.

Maria broke down in tears and went to get a bottle of spirits from the local store. She drank it, and having believed what the men had to say, and not realizing the situation never bothered to phone her friend up.

Annette practiced yoga for a few days and binged on chocolate. She was short of money and went back to work, where she washed currants to make malt loaves for a local bakery. The two men, Ronnie and Paul got on with their jobs and thought little of the incident over the weekend.

Maria went crazy for a week. To top everything off her daughter turned up on the Thursday and said she was having Ryan's baby and had been thrown out of his parent's home because no-one there wanted her to have it. Maria said to her daughter, "Not at the moment. You'll have to get out of here as well".

Not knowing where to go, Marissa went to Annette's house and managed to persuade her to give up her couch until she had found somewhere permanent. They talked and tried to phone Maria, to see if she had calmed down and whether the situation could be sorted out. Maria was not answering the phone, and Annette and Marissa did not see her until the

On the Bright Side

following weekend when they all turned up at the same pub in the town center by chance.

The sight of her daughter and the woman who had shagged her boyfriend was too much for Maria. She went ballistic and attacked Annette, not listening to what she had to say. Her daughter tried to drag her off Annette, but on being punched in the face left them to it. Annette was smaller and weaker but fought back. The two women tumbled over the cobbled courtyard of the town-center pub.

Maria was on top of Annette, who was trying to poke her eyes off in an attempt to get her off. Having seen a broken beer glass by the side of a chair within reach Maria grabbed it and blindly shoved it into the face of Annette. Everything had happened within the space of a minute and the bouncers then appeared on the scene. They grabbed Maria and disabled her, calling the police who were never far away from the town-center on a Friday night. Maria looked at Annette's face, horrified at what she had done and beginning to think of what was going to happen to her. The two women left, one in an ambulance and the other in a police van. Maria was charged with grievous bodily harm and taken to Styal prison in Cheshire.

Maria got on well in prison and was let out with half her sentence done three years later. She met her daughter, who was waiting at the gates. Maria broke down in tears at seeing her grandson for the first time and her daughter asked her how she was. She replied, "Alcohol free, drug free and ready to be a better mother". Maria asked how Annette was and was told her friend would never talk to her again. She asked about Ronnie and Paul to be told Ronnie was in prison for murder and Paul for drug-smuggling. She said, "Serves the bastards right". Maria and her daughter went home to a council flat in another area of Manchester and never looked back.

Andrew Aldred

John Thomas

John Thomas' friend Michael appeared at the door. John opened it and let him in. They had their customary cup of tea and went to church in Michael's jaguar. They were old friends from public school and had both had successful careers, John having been a banker and Michael going into textiles. They lived on the same street, in an upmarket area of Bloxham, near Oxfordshire. It was quiet and secluded and the houses had their own large gardens. Needless to say, they were both keen gardeners. They arrived at church, an Anglican one at the end of a cul-de-sac near the town center. They had both been to that church for as long as they could remember, which was a very long time. John took Sunday school there, taking an interest in the children and having been a scoutmaster for a significant part of his life.

It was here that John met Amy for the first time. She was an innocent and pretty girl, or so John thought, if a bit simple and overly childish for her age. She had just turned fourteen. She lived in a council estate a few streets away from John. By chance she learned his address, which she noted.

Amy took to walking past John Thomas' house quite often in the hope she might see him and get invited in. She felt sure this rich old man could give her what she wanted, which was sex and some pocket money. She thought John good-looking for his age, a damn sight better than his friend Michael. Her mother had frequent relationships with different men and she did not see why she could not do the same. She had seduced some of the boys in her class at school and was ready for something else in her life. Amy's school was a school for "educationally subnormal" children, who are now termed as having "learning difficulties".

John was in his garden one day, and seeing Amy passing by had a chat with her and let her in his house for a cup of tea. John's wife had been dead for a few years and he was a

On the Bright Side

lonely man who thought himself too late in life for another relationship. As John got the tea Amy loosened the buttons of her blouse to reveal her well-developed breasts and hitched up her skirt a little. She was confident for a girl of her age and sat next to John who quickly caught on and seized his opportunity when she puckered her lips up for a kiss. They began to fumble with each other and after saying "God forgive me for what I am about to do", John had sex with the fourteen-year-old girl on the rug in front of his fireplace, regretting it as soon as he had. How was he going to cover this up? He had a reputation to uphold and a considerable social standing in the local community.

John did not see Amy for a few weeks after that and when she turned up and told him she was pregnant he nearly died in his chair. He made her a meal that day and asked her whether anyone knew where she was, and receiving the answer that they didn't, he thought of a plan. As they sat together on the settee, John said he thought she should be going and asked her for a kiss. As she responded John grabbed her by the throat and throttled her with his hands. She tried to struggle but it was no use. He choked her to death in a couple of minutes. John hid her out of sight in his spare room and waited for nightfall. He got his gardening clothes on at eleven-o-clock and began to dig a hole in his garden for her body. The soil in John's garden was of good quality and in a few hours he had dug a grave for her that went six feet down. He covered her in bleach to disguise the smell of the body, and putting her in the hole began to fill it. After he had done this he went to buy some roses for his new "flower bed" the following morning. Nobody heard anything in John's secluded garden and no-one suspected anything. John went for a drink in the local pub the following day to steady his nerves and waited to see if anybody had noticed anything. He read about her disappearance in the paper, and thought the police might come round to interview him but they never did. He was above suspicion, a well-respected and decent member of the community. He went about his business and acted as if nothing had happened.

Andrew Aldred

Some years later John Thomas was diagnosed with Parkinson's disease and Alzheimer's. Michael had to call John Thomas' son, a Major in the army to get his father admitted to a local hospital after John was caught wandering the streets at night in his pajamas talking nonsense. John died shortly after this, and was buried at the local cemetery in a grave with a large marble tombstone. His house was sold to a family with an increasing number of children. One day they decided to build an extension on their house. The builders came with a JCB and dug up the flower bed where Amy was buried. There was local outrage but Amy's mother said she was just glad to find the body of her daughter and give her a decent burial. Amy was buried in the same cemetery as John but in a different area.

On a Sunday shortly after Amy's burial her mother was in the graveyard putting some flowers on Amy's grave. She walked round the graveyard to have a look at the other graves and noticed one had been smashed with what must have been a sledgehammer. She noted the name "John Thomas" and smiled wryly to herself.

On the Bright Side

Killing in the Name of Religion

Malcolm loosened the tourniquet as the drug entered his bloodstream. He took the needle out of his arm and put his works away in the bedside cabinet. He felt the presence of God all around him, as if someone had turned a light on inside him. He lay back and thought of his religion and how blessed he was.

Malcolm then took his artists knife out of the cabinet and cut himself to feel the pain and power of God. The heroin and the self-harm helped him connect with his God and made him feel special. The staff called him through the door, asking him if he wanted any tea and he replied that he didn't because he had eaten whilst he was out.

He lived in a hostel for the mentally ill, somewhere between Manchester and Bolton. He had a dark past and had spent some considerable time in prison and then in secure mental hospital.

The staff did not take much notice of Malcolm. They thought he was ok because he believed in God and also went to Church on a Sunday to worship. They believed that his religious beliefs and the church would keep him under control. They knew about his heroin addiction but did not think he posed a threat to anyone and thought him sane and repentant.

Malcolm was not, however, sane or repentant. He was a hard-line Christian who believed in the bible literally and to the letter. He believed in hell-fire and damnation, Noah's ark, the feeding of the five thousand and all the other stories which most people would take with a pinch of salt and look for a deeper meaning in. To Malcolm it was all God's honest truth, in short, gospel.

Malcolm had served twenty years in prison for killing a woman he had sex with because she was a liar and a prostitute and had passed on her social diseases. She had also ridiculed him for the size of his penis, which was less than average.

Andrew Aldred

He had found God in his cell after taking heroin and had never connected his drug habits with his belief in God and the bible. Instead of being repentant Malcolm thought his connection with God vindicated him of his crime. He had been transferred to mental hospital, but was thought of as no longer being a threat because of his age and the fact he had done nothing violent in recent years. All the same, he had done his time and nobody gets locked up forever without good reason. He was in some ways a friendly person, and always willing to talk about God and the bible, his favourite subject.

Malcolm kept to himself a lot. He would listen to his Christian rock music and he took his medication early that night, as usual. He woke up the next morning and went to the paper shop for his tobacco, getting on with his life the best way he could.

Malcolm got out of bed feeling half-dead as usual and got dressed. His clothes weren't up to much. He wore a donkey jacket and capped boots and jeans that were getting more worn by the minute and had a patch where they had gone through at the left knee. He had a tattoo of God on his left forearm and a large cross on his right one and was quite fit for forty-five, well-built and physically active. He had a smoke in the yard at the hostel, eat his breakfast at the appointed time speaking to a member of the female staff to say he was alright and walked out of the building to get his tobacco for the day.

He had made something of a friend of the shopkeeper, an Asian man called Ramesh, who seemed quite content for Malcolm to talk to him about Christianity and very Western in his outlook. Malcolm thought he might one day be able to convert Ramesh to Christianity and save his Muslim soul.

Ramesh, on the other hand, had an ulterior motive for putting up with Malcolm. He could see that Malcolm was an isolated and vulnerable figure in some ways and wanted to have sex with this rather ignorant Christian man who was always stopping to talk to him in his shop. Ramesh had not

On the Bright Side

come on to Malcolm yet but was working on a way past Malcolm's religious fervour to corner him into having a gay relationship.

Ramesh had always had ideas of being a woman's hairdresser and running a shop of his own, but due to lack of funds had ended up running his parent's paper shop whilst his devout Muslim parents carried on with other things. Both of Ramesh's parents understood he was a bit "different" in some ways, although they would advocate he was as manly as anyone else. Ramesh did not follow Islam and dressed in a Western European way, wearing cowboy boots and some cheaper designer brands of clothing. Ramesh had no desire to make his sexuality public and was quite content to carry on his life as it was and have the occasional short relationship with anyone of the same sex under the guise of friendship. He had invited Malcolm to visit him that night to have some Asian food in the flat at the shop after he had closed it up.

After agreeing to meet Ramesh later on, Malcolm went to Manchester to visit his drug dealer at a pub near the town centre, on the way to the Strangeways prison.

Malcolm caught the bus with his free pass and enjoyed the journey through Salford. The withdrawal from last night's fix had not set in yet and his medication dulled the symptoms considerably. Malcolm had unlimited leave at the hostel although he was not allowed to sleep anywhere else. He was nearing the end of his stay at the hostel and would shortly be moved to a shared house to continue his recovery. He got off the bus at the Arndale and walked down Shudehill towards where his dealer was waiting for him. Steve Black, or black-market Steve was a psychopathic ex-corporal from the Parachute Regiment who had been thrown out for drug-dealing and violence and showed no signs of changing his ways. Malcolm was wary of people in Manchester, and particularly of black-market Steve. He stopped at Stensby's gun shop and eyed up some knives. There was a flick knife with a wooden handle going for a tenner and after some thought Malcolm went in and bought it, stuffing it inside his sock before he went out.

Andrew Aldred

He then went on a short walk to the dive bar where Steve hung out.

Steve greeted Malcolm at the bar with his usual biker's death grip handshake, squeezing Malcolm's hand uncomfortably hard and not letting go whilst putting his other arm around him and escorting him to a table. He grunted "Show me the money" to Malcolm, who got his money out and hoped he wasn't about to be ripped off. Luckily Steve was in a good mood that day made better by the fact he was slightly drunk, having been there for a few hours already. The money disappeared into Steve's bulging wallet and he pulled out a small plastic packet from another pocket which contained Malcolm's drugs. Steve said "Good to you, aren't I?" and followed it up with "Well, get out of here" as he laughed and went to the bar to get another pint. Malcolm got up and walked towards the door. He heard Steve shout at him "You're a good boy" as he thought what a bastard Steve was and how he had spent twenty years in prison to get treated like this. He got out of the pub and walked quickly back to the Arndale bus station. He had known Steve a long time and had only stuck with him because Steve had not ripped him off yet, but the only reason Steve had not ripped him off was because he knew Malcolm would be back and there was money to be made.

He got on the bus back to Bolton and started to look forward to taking his drugs after he had seen Ramesh that night. He was looking forward to some Asian food.

Malcolm arrived at his stop, halfway between the hostel and the paper shop and walked through the village where he lived to the shop, which had its shutters up. He knocked on the door and waited. After about a minute Ramesh appeared and let him in. They went upstairs and Ramesh heated up a curry left for them by his mother in the microwave. They ate the curry and started to talk.

Ramesh steered the subject towards homosexuality and stated that in his eyes buggery was an act of friendship between two men. Malcolm did not agree and cited instances in the bible where homosexuals were stoned to

On the Bright Side

death. They started to argue and Ramesh said he was gay and he wanted to have sex with Malcolm, who should be grateful because of his lower social status and because he did not know anybody else in the area. Malcolm said he would tell Ramesh's parents that their son was a homosexual and tried to walk out. A fight broke out between the two men and they tumbled downstairs and reaching the ground floor started to make a mess of the shop as they wrestled and fought. Ramesh stood in front of the door, denying Malcolm his escape and seemed to have gained the upper hand in the fight, being younger and stronger. Malcolm remembered his flick knife and grabbed it out of his sock whilst Ramesh stood in his way. Ramesh did not recognise the blade as what it was and by the time the knife had sprung out of its handle it was too late. Malcolm stabbed his friend three times, puncturing both lungs and leaving a wound in his abdomen. He then told his friend to pray to Jesus Christ for forgiveness as he walked out of the shop. He closed the door and seeing a bus coming around the corner got on it and went to Bolton.

Ramesh, in the mean-time tried to phone his mother but could not speak and collapsed and died on the shop counter. His mother looked up who had phoned her and she and her husband went down to see their son's dead body. They phoned the police who started making enquiries about Malcolm, who had not returned to the hostel that evening.

Malcolm stopped in a few bars to drown his sorrows that evening. He had considered his situation and the last place he wanted to be going was back to prison but he knew that was what he was facing. He slept in a multi-story car park that night and was glad for the fact that he had brought his works with him and could take his heroin. Somehow his trip that night was different. There was no religious and no presence from God. All the drug did was give him some relaxation and some sleep. He slept in the lift and was woken up by a policeman the following day. The officer was on his own and Malcolm overpowered him and ran up the stairs towards the roof. The officer called for back-up after realising who he had cornered and Malcolm found himself cornered on the top of the building. He jumped onto the wall

Andrew Aldred

and stood facing the police officers who told him to come down and everything would be alright and they would look after him. Malcolm knew they were lying and jumped, screaming "God take me". He closed his eyes on the way down and imagined a huge hand scooping him up. When he opened his eyes all he could see was the ground approaching and his last thought was that God had deserted him.

On the Bright Side

The Fugitive Rapist

It was time for tea again in the secure unit. John hoped he would not be missed as he struggled with the window that he was gradually removing from the wall next to the roof in the dormitory. He had scraped away with a blunt penknife at the mortar for the last few months whilst the rest of them were having their meals and put the window back as it was filling the cracks with toothpaste. The job was nearly done and John filled the holes he had made in the mortar and plaster with his tube of Macleans and lay on his bed thinking of freedom and what he was going to do. The window that John was removing had a wooden frame and had plastic glass which was screwed into the frame. John had no screwdriver and had realized the only way to freedom was to remove the entire window, frame and all. He switched his stereo on and listened to No Limit by Two Unlimited for the thousandth time while they finished tea and came back to the dormitory or went to the smoke room to get a dose of lung abuse.

John had found the penknife on one of his trips out with his Occupational Therapist, Sarah. He had picked it up unnoticed from the seat of a tram. It was a thin, two bladed knife that suited his purpose very well. He had saved up what was to John a handsome sum of money whilst he had been in Prestwich hospital out of his allowance for toiletries and tobacco. John did not smoke except for smoking drugs, which he had not done for a while. This made the money in his wallet build up a lot quicker. All he had to buy was his toiletries, and of course lots of toothpaste. No one had ever pulled up John about buying toothpaste. They all thought he was a bit simple and incapable of much. John was aware of this and played the fool for them whilst he got on with getting out of his situation, which he was not happy with.

John decided that it was safe to come out and went to watch television with the other folk. Coronation Street and Emmerdale were on and he needed to relax and hope no one was going to realize what he was planning until he was gone.

Andrew Aldred

A few days later the window finally came out and John decided he would be gone that night. He put it back and went to watch television with everyone else. No one noticed that John was in a better mood than normal and no one cared.

The night staff usually came to check the dormitories at about one o clock for the final time before they settled into their night of trying to sort out their own problems and everyone else's in the chairs between the dormitories at the bottom of the corridor. John's dormitory was at the top of the corridor and he was considered a low risk patient although he had come from prison and not been there long.

John waited until two o clock and got his clothes on while the rest of the dormitory happily snored. He scraped away with his penknife in the dark, stopping when anyone rolled over in bed or made any sort of noise. At three o clock he was ready. He took the window out and placed it under the covers of the bed, crawling on to the roof. He felt like a cat burglar and the thought gave him immense satisfaction. Keeping out of the lights surrounding the building he navigated the roof until he reached a point he could jump to the ground. It was twenty feet up and John eased himself down as far as he could get, falling backwards and away from the wall to the ground. He slowly got up and checked no one was around. Then he skirted around the car park keeping out of the light and went up the back lane grinning to himself. He was out.

John climbed on the late night bus at the top of the road and went to Manchester to have a pint at a bar he had not been in for a long time knowing he would not be recognized. He then walked to Piccadilly Railway Station and took an early morning train to Alderley Edge, on the other side of Manchester hoping to get away as far as he could before he was noticed.

John arrived in Alderley Edge and started looking for a residential place to hide out in. He needed a house with a shed in the garden that was unlocked. He found a housing estate and lo and behold, there was a shed left unlocked.

On the Bright Side

John went into the shed and lay down, exhausted. He pulled the door to and slept until the following night. John woke up hungry and disoriented. He realized where he was and that it was night time. He opened the shed door gently and slipped outside, noticing lights on in the house whose shed he had borrowed the previous night. He saw a couple through the back window having a drink of lager and finishing a takeaway meal. He was immediately jealous of their cozy, insulated lifestyle and decided to look further around their property. He noticed that they had three cars, one for him, a BMW saloon, one for her, a small Peugeot, and also a Peugeot 306, an older car that seemed to John exactly what he wanted for the next stage of his getaway.

John waited in their garden for a long time, and the man came out of the house with the empty bottles of beer and the remnants of the takeaway food to put it in the bin. John waited in the shadows for a chance to get in the kitchen. The woman wanted the man of the house to go to bed with her. "He's in luck" thought John, "And maybe I am". The man went upstairs to see to his wife and John crept in the kitchen and did not waste time in looking for car keys. All the keys to the house and cars were on some hooks near the kettle and John studied the keys, noting that the more recent ones were cut a different way. He seized the keys to the old Peugeot, and took a couple of bags of crisps from a bowl that was on the kitchen table. John crept outside again and waited in the shadows. The man duly came down half an hour afterwards and locked the door. John spent another night in the shed. He hoped that tomorrow was a week day and they would be at work so he could continue his escape. John laughed to himself as he lay in the shed. He was enjoying himself immensely.

As John sleeps, no doubt dreaming of girls in some pole dancing club doing vulgar things, lets tell you a bit about him.

John has aspirations of being a boxer. He has had some success as an amateur fighting for Amir Khan's gym in Bolton, and since being kicked out for being drunk and stoned when he turned up for training has been doing

Andrew Aldred

sporadic training at a gym in Ardwick in Manchester. All of this was of course before he wound up in prison and mental hospital for smashing up his uncle's house where he had lived. John's mother was a junkie and incapable of looking after him and his dad was in long term prison for a series of serious crimes. John worked in a nightclub in Bury, where he lived, collecting glasses and had developed a taste for alcohol whilst doing this. After a couple of weeks of him turning up drunk at the house and waking him up his uncle had booted him out of the house. John did not go without a fight and was duly charged with assault and criminal damage. After a few months in Strangeways prison in Manchester, John was transferred to Prestwich mental hospital. John had been born in 1995 and it was now spring of 2015. He would turn twenty later on this year.

John was quite vain. He liked designer clothes and spent all his time collecting what he could from second hand shops. He wore a Lonsdale hoodie and Bench jeans. He had bought his Nike trainers brand new and used to do his roadwork for boxing in them. He was normally clean shaven, but had some slight stubble since his breakout. He was good looking and had an athletic build, with no tattoos or visible marks. He would normally wear aftershave and deodorant, and even if the ladies did not always fancy him, he fancied himself as a whole lot of things.
John got up quite early the next morning and lay in wait for the occupiers of the house to go to work. He heard the BMW starting and pulling off and out of the drive and knew it was just the lady of the house he had to wait for. He came out of the shed being careful not to be noticed and hid behind a hedge in the garden. He could see her from the shadows having a cup of coffee in the kitchen. She was about fifty and looked her age. John thought "Not for me!" as the woman finished her coffee and did the washing up from breakfast. She got her coat from the back of a chair and John knew that she was on her way out. She got in her car and drove away, unsuspecting.

John came out of hiding and got into the Peugeot 306. The street was quiet and John took advantage of this to look at where everything was on the dashboard, and turning the key

On the Bright Side

in the ignition realized he had picked a winner. The car had three quarters of a tank of petrol in it as well.

John had not passed his driving test but was a reasonably competent driver. His uncle had taken him out on a disused air field a few times and let him drive his van. He had also driven other cars illegally, although he was not a habitual car thief.

John pulled out of the drive and turned left. He realized he would have to get used to driving this car before he went where he wanted to go and headed out of Alderley Edge to the surrounding countryside. He drove around for half an hour and stopped for a cup of coffee and a sandwich at a garage. He drove around for a bit longer and saw an exit for the motorway. He was ready.

John entered the motorway and headed for the M6. He was careful not to go too fast and stayed in the inside lane whilst he gained his confidence driving. The drugs the hospital had given him were beginning to wear off and he felt liberated and ultimately free. He reached for the radio and turned it on. It was playing "Beds are burning" by Midnight Oil. The lyrics "It belongs to them, let's give it back" and "let's pay the rent, let's pay our share" did not cut any ice with John. He turned it off and concentrated on driving. He knew where he was going. He wanted to head for North Wales where he had been youth hosteling with friends a few years ago. He exited the M6 and took the M56, deciding that he could actually overtake a few cars. John decided to stop just outside Wales at a service station. There was a "Starbucks" there and he got a coffee and sat out with the other guests. He felt like he was someone for the first time in his life. He was in a car, going about his business like everyone else. For once in his life, he did not feel like a loser. He headed through Queensferry and Mold to a place called Llangollen, where he had stayed with friends from school a few years ago. John stopped at the convenience store in the village to buy some cans of lager and a couple of pasties, and parked his stolen car up near the hostel he had planned to stay at. John had not planned his existence outside the hospital beyond this point and was starting to think about what he would have to do to survive and how he would have to make his money. He had realized what he had got into and that his life was now that of a fugitive. He went back to the convenience store and bought some razors and some deodorant, thinking it was in his best interests to at least look respectable. Then he walked into the hostel where he had stayed as a teenager and booked a bed in the hostel.

It was here that John met the girl that would bring about his downfall. John was having a cup of tea in the common room at the hostel when three girls walked in. Two of them were a bit overweight and seemed to get on better with each other than the third who was skinny and had purple hair. The two overweight girls introduced themselves as Joanne and Patricia, and the one with the purple hair, who John had his eye on introduced herself as Lisa. Joanne and Patricia wanted to walk into the village and have an underage couple of pints while Lisa wanted to stay behind, hoping to get to know the handsome stranger in the common room a bit better. She said she had been walking with her friends on the River Dee walks, a local attraction. The River Dee went all the way back to Liverpool, where they were all from. They were school friends on holiday and Lisa was thinking it might be the last time they were all together as a group, as the two other, slightly older girls were going to sixth form college and Lisa did not know what she was going to do next year. She was the youngest in the class, being fifteen years of age and still a virgin, which she could not admit to and desperately wanted to be rid of.

John gave her a load of bullshit about himself, saying he was a promising young boxer from Manchester and had just won the area championship. He gave her his real name though, which was a big mistake. After they had talked for some small amount of time John reached over and put his tongue in her mouth. He had not had sex for a long time and was desperate for it, and suggested that they have a shower together. Lisa, desperate to please, and young and impressionable accepted the invitation.

On the Bright Side

When they got to the shower John had ripped his clothes off in seconds flat, Lisa taking not much longer, and they got to grips with each other, Lisa noticing how powerful and strong John was. At first she found this sexy, but as John let the beast in him loose, she struggled to be free. John was having none of it and the more she struggled the more it turned him on. He shot his load and let her go. She immediately rushed out of the shower and to her room. She started crying on her bed and realized what a let-down her first real sexual experience had been. John finished his shower and got dressed, quite oblivious to what he had done to the young girl. He then rested on his bed, delighted that he had got his end away that evening. Lisa, meanwhile decided to do something about the situation and put her clothes on. She then went to the village to find her friends. Joanne and Patricia were enjoying their second pint of cider when Lisa found them in the local pub. They were horrified and furious. The girls went to confront John and burst into his room, grabbing hold of him as he lay with his eyes shut. No-one was in the mood to talk and the two girls laid into John while Lisa stood in the background. John struggled to his feet and started to fight back, using his boxing skills and punching both girls hard and accurately as they tried to overpower him. John was too strong for them and they could not hold him. He waded through them and Lisa into the hallway and ran out past the housekeeper, who wanted to know what was going on. John got in the stolen car and drove off while the three girls poured their hearts out to the bewildered woman who kept the hostel. After a few minutes the police were called and informed of John's name and some vague details of the car he was driving. John, in the mean-time had realized he had done something wrong and was driving away from the scene like the clappers.

The police came to the hostel and took statements from all concerned, then putting a message on the local radio about John, saying he should not be approached and to inform the police of his whereabouts.

John drove through mid-Wales, stopping once for petrol and a sandwich. He paid for the petrol and walked out of the garage, but the woman serving at the counter had clocked

Andrew Aldred

him and informed the police which direction he was heading in. John was beginning to get psychotic with withdrawal from his psychiatric medication and was obviously not in a good frame of mind. This showed in his driving as well as his general demeanor.

John sped up the road towards Aberystwyth. It was half-past ten at night and dark. Suddenly John saw headlights in front of him. There were two pairs of them and they were stationary. The road was blocked and he jammed on his brakes, screeching to a halt yards in front of a police van and a Range Rover. Another police vehicle drove behind him, boxing him in and half a dozen police men approached his stolen car. They dragged him out of it, gave him a well-deserved kicking and hauled him off to Ruthin jail after they had charged him. John woke up the next morning to be seen by a solicitor and a psychiatrist, neither of whom had any sympathy for him. He also had a court appearance and realized he was in a hell of a lot of trouble. That night three prison officers came to visit John in his cell. They called him Johnny English, a name that stuck with him while he was in Ruthin and gave him a severe beating. As they walked out of his cell, one of them said, "Welcome to Wales".

The solicitor had told John that he would spend a number of years in Ashworth High Security Hospital in Liverpool and given him a list of all his charges, telling him there was no other option. The psychiatrist had briefly interviewed him, saying very little and John realized that he might never get out this time. Ashworth was a very heavy place and he dreaded going there. He had hated being at Prestwich Hospital. The other prisoners were very unsympathetic and unimpressed by John and he had no family or friends.

That night he ripped his bedsheet up into a long strip, tying one end to his neck and the other to the door handle in his cell. He fought back the tears, crouched against the door and let his body fall. He had measured it so that there was just enough ground clearance for him to break his neck. He saw white light and then blackness and that was the last memory he had of this world. John was buried at the local cemetery shortly afterwards in an unmarked grave in

On the Bright Side

unconsecrated ground. No-one came to his funeral and nobody missed him.

Andrew Aldred

The Pagan Woman

Margaret relaxed in the conservatory that afternoon as she usually did. She took the Pagan mirror with its gold surround, like an old fashioned Sun God off the wall and looked into it. She saw an old and discontented woman. She remembered her youth and her mother and wistfully put the mirror back where it belonged.

Margaret and Geoffrey lived in a remote farmhouse in Wales. It was somewhere between Aberystwyth and Cardiff, and there are many miles of open countryside between these two towns.

They were a childless couple, both in their seventies and had retired to their country house, which was five miles from the nearest neighbor. They had planned to see out their last years there. They had worked as a husband and wife team of solicitors, him being the boss, and she his secretary. They had lived near Birmingham and taken care of many a divorce and court battle in their time.

Geoffrey did most of the work around the farmhouse, as he had done in their firm of solicitors. He collected firewood to burn on their open stove, grew vegetables and kept livestock, two pigs and some chickens. Margaret looked after the house and did the cooking, but there was a growing discontent in her. Geoffrey was growing older and turning to drink for his relaxation. It was all he did in the evening until he fell asleep next to his whisky bottle.

She had always been happy for him to be in charge, but now she felt he was not fit for that. She felt increasingly ignored and unloved. The only interest she had was the television and being in a remote area of South Wales, the reception was not very good.

Geoffrey went to the nearest town that day to get provisions. A case of whisky for him, some bars of chocolate for her, some fresh bread, butter, sugar, milk and very little else.

On the Bright Side

They were sat in front of the television that night relaxing, him with his bottle beside him and her on the other side of the room in their respective armchairs.

Margaret spoke to her husband for the first time in a couple of months. She complained about their love life, that he never showed her any affection and that she felt ignored, and at the situation in the farmhouse, miles from anywhere without any social contact. Geoffrey said nothing. He was too old to make love to his wife and was content with his life as it was. He went back to his whisky and Margaret determined to do something about her situation and her unhappy life. What she did was probably not the right thing to do but it was all she could think of. She waited until he had fallen asleep in his chair and got a long, thin knife out of the rack in the kitchen. She placed it where his heart was and drove it through his rib cage. He scarcely moved and did not even wake up. She said to the corpse, "You were dead anyway. Dead to me!" She removed the knife and finished the bottle of whisky by his side and thought what to do with his body. That night the moon was full. She watched it for hours and thought how she would continue her revenge on her dead husband.

The following day she dragged him into the kitchen. There was not much blood and she cleaned up where he had been. She cut his clothes off and burned them in the incinerator. Then she got a meat cleaver and a saw and cut his body into joints of meat. She cut his penis off and bagged the meat up, putting it in the freezer. The rest of his body and his head she fed to the pigs. She smiled as they set about devouring their former master and set about cooking his testicles and penis for her breakfast with a couple of fried eggs. She was enjoying being in charge and the fact that she was going to eat her husband was a huge joke to her. She looked at the mirror in the conservatory and smiled to herself. She thought of her mother and how amused she would be at the recent turn of events for her and Geoffrey.

Andrew Aldred

During the next month Margaret systematically ate Geoffrey, enjoying her revenge on him. She cooked up his body with vegetables from the garden and drank his whisky at night, not seeing a soul. She was quite delighted at her grim secret.

One day she woke up with a pain on the right side of her stomach. It got gradually worse and she decided she would have to go to the nearest village to see the doctor. She tried to start the Land Rover up but the vehicle had not been used for a month and the battery was flat. She decided to call for an ambulance but the telephone line had blown down in a recent storm and had not been fixed.

She struggled to get back to the car as the pain worsened, getting in and trying to start it. She felt the pain spreading as her appendix burst and she lay bent over the steering wheel in the drivers' seat. She came to a decision and reached into the glove compartment. She would not be able to get help and would die anyway. She took her husband's knife out and sat up with some effort. She gathered herself and cut her own throat.

Sometime later a local shepherd came across the deserted farmhouse, looking for a stray sheep and saw the dead body slumped over the steering wheel. The police were informed and a suicide verdict was quickly reached. Nobody ever found out what had happened to her husband.

On the Bright Side

War Games

Vinnie got off the bus at his new home, a training Regiment for the British army in Yorkshire. That day he picked up his kit, polished his boots and missed his mother and father, but he knew he could not be at home and not work forever, so he had enlisted with the Infantry and today he began his military career.

The following day, the Sergeant Major took the troop for drill. Vinnie fell about laughing at this giant of a man who seemed as though he had a pole up his arse, he was so delighted with himself as he marched up and down with his pay stick. Vinnie got sent to jail for that, having to lift a tank shell up and down for half an hour until his arms felt like jelly. He was then allowed to re-join the troop.

Vinnie was small and slightly built. He was tough and good-looking though and he was not about to give up on the only chance he had in this world of being something. He was twenty years old and had never had a job before, and this was an opportunity for him. He had always worked on his fitness, being an amateur football player and a good runner. He found himself fitter than the other lads in the troop and good at the battle marches, carrying a rifle and full kit, although he struggled in the gym because he had to train with people bigger and stronger than himself, and a lot of the training involved fighting skills and using the body weight of the person you were training with.

Vinnie was from Manchester, East Manchester to be precise. He had not had an easy upbringing and did not take shit from the other lads in the troop or the corporals, a fact which would later on be held against him.

The troop went out on its first exercise in Dartmoor that November. They started proceedings by attacking a hill individually. They tried to get to the top of it to see some information and were taken prisoner by the corporals as they made their way up the hill. The exercise took place in the dark. Some of the lads went full pelt at the corporals, trying to get past them but Vinnie hid in the undergrowth, trying to get closer by stealth until he could see the information the corporals were hiding. All of a sudden they wrapped this activity up but Vinnie did not know they had. He was hiding in some undergrowth towards the top of the hill and remained there because the corporals had not caught him. Vinnie re-joined the rest of the troop ten minutes later when he realised what was going on, only to get assaulted by his corporal for not falling in with the other lads. The corporal beat the smaller man up leaving Vinnie in a heap after head-butting him several times. Undeterred, Vinnie carried on with the exercise, only to get singled out by the corporal again, this time being kissed and groped in front of the troop. Vinnie bottled his pride and got on with the job.

On the second exercise they went to Wales, and this went a lot better for Vinnie. He was good at the battle drills and the basic infantry tactics, and walked and ran all day in the Welsh forests without complaint. Vinnie passed the exercise with a "B" grade and progressed to the third and final exercise he had to complete before he joined the Regiment.

This was the advanced Infantry drills, and included section attacks using live rounds, and also digging battle trenches in a hillside that was full of rocks and slate. Vinnie got off to a bad start, when his rifle did not clear after he had finished an exercise on the ranges, and he let off a bullet into the ground when he was unloading his rifle. The corporal got one of the bigger lads to empty a mess tin full of food over Vinnie's head whilst they ate. Vinnie was fuming. The rifle had not cleared when it should have done and he had done everything right. Vinnie mouthed off to one of the lads that he would like to shoot the corporal which was something that he should not have done. This was taken seriously, although it was just bravado as far as Vinnie was concerned. All he wanted was to be treated with a little bit of respect as he tried to get through the exercise and pass it. The corporal pushed Vinnie into a river later on that day. It was the middle of January and Vinnie froze all day while on exercise. When the corporal said, "Who's a bastard?" to Vinnie, he replied, "You are, corporal", which went down like a lead balloon. The corporal hit Vinnie hard in the solar

On the Bright Side

plexus and kicked him over. Vinnie picked himself up and got on with things as he usually did.

That was the end of their week and everyone was going out on Friday night to get drunk and try it on with the local girls. Vinnie went down with everyone else and had a skin-full. He saw the corporal in one of the pubs and could not resist opening his mouth. "Don't fuck him, he's bald!", said Vinnie. This was the icing on the cake for the corporal and his mates. They had a quiet word about Vinnie and agreed they did not want him to pass out with the rest of the troop and go to Ireland the following month. One of the corporals bought Vinnie a drink, a pint of orange juice to supposedly sober up. In fact, it was a pint of vodka with a small quantity of orange juice in it. Unsuspecting, Vinnie drank the drink that had been bought for him and promptly collapsed. He had to be taken home in the back of the troop officer's car. He was then dealt with under the jurisdiction of the troop staff. They stripped him of his trousers and underpants, bent him over the bed and raped him. Vinnie woke up the following morning and went on parade, still drunk and not knowing what had happened. One of the lads let on to Vinnie. The following day they went on exercise again.

They did live section attacks down a valley and up the other side of it. Vinnie was detailed to give covering fire, which he did. He watched the corporal's beret as they went down the hill, easy to distinguish because the rest of the troop were in helmets. Vinnie thought about shooting the corporal, but he didn't. The troop came back and the corporal asked why Vinnie had not followed the rest of them down the hill. Vinnie replied that he was asked to give covering fire and not called forward so that's what he did. The corporal called Vinnie a coward and Vinnie exploded. He raised his weapon to point it at the corporal, and as he opened his mouth to speak the sergeant shot him in the back. The bullet ripped through Vinnie, leaving him dead with a hole the size of a small plate in his chest.

The sergeant said to the corporal, "This thing has gone far enough". The corporal asked, "What do you want me to do?" The sergeant said, "As far as I'm concerned he was

Andrew Aldred

killed on exercise by a stray bullet. He'll be given a full military send off. If I hear of any more trouble from you, you will be next. Understand?" The corporal said, "Yes, sergeant". Vinnie was given a decent burial and his parents were informed and went to attend. Vinnie's dad suspected more had went on than the army admitted but they closed ranks on him. All he could do was make sure his youngest son did not follow in Vinnie's footsteps and join the army.

On the Bright Side

Wasting Time

Dr Moore worked in the Alpha Unit. This was a secure accommodation unit for the mentally ill somewhere between Bolton and Bury. He prided himself on being more psychopathic than any of the patients and not allowing any of them to break his will. He was a stocky man with round, horn-rimmed glasses. His life was based around his job and he had very little interest in anything else. He was divorced, his wife being the only person who had ever disputed anything with him and got away with it, and she had a considerable amount of money for doing so.

Dr Moore was waiting in his office to see Dean, who was a small-time gangster and drug-dealer. Dean had the mistaken idea that street drugs were good for him and that society needed to make space for people like him to do whatever they wanted in it. Dean was a complete waste of space, in other words, who could not see society or reality for what it was and had no intention of conforming to anything to do with society or reality.

They had the same conversation as they had done in previous weeks, Dr Moore saying that they knew Dean had taken drugs, mainly cocaine and ecstasy, and he should subscribe to the drugs the hospital was supplying him with because he would get better and stop feeling ill because he was over-loaded with the drugs the hospital had been giving him and what he had been taking himself. Dean screamed, "You're trying to kill me, you bastard!", before being hauled off by two burly male nurses to a room where he could be watched over for his own good and everyone else's.

After another week of "close observations", Dean was allowed to re-join the rest of the ward, and promptly went back to taking drugs. He hated Dr Moore and could see the fundamental disagreement between them would never get any better. He began to look for a weapon to settle his score with this doctor, who did not seem to hear a word he said, and had the same conversation every bloody week with him. When the maintenance men were mending a door, he managed to get his hands on a screwdriver they

Andrew Aldred

had taken their eyes off for a minute or two. He then thought how he could get close to Dr Moore.

It was Thursday again, and time for Dean and Dr Moore to have their weekly conversation. Dean agreed with what the doctor had to say this week, confusing everybody, including the doctor, who still seemed to disbelieve him, but also acknowledged that this was a significant step in the right direction. The doctor sat in a chair behind his desk with Dean directly in front of him. Dr Moore was flanked by two male nurses. All of a sudden Dean leaped at the doctor, pulling the screwdriver from up his sleeve where he had hidden it. Dean knew he would only have the chance for one blow as the nurses immediately began to respond to his actions. The doctor had covered his head with his hands, and as he got dragged off the desk, Dean picked his spot and buried the screwdriver in it. The alarms went off and Dean was hauled off to seclusion again, leaving the doctor with the screwdriver stuck in his head, where it had pierced his brain and killed him.

Dean was given the "liquid cosh" by a third nurse, and as he lay unconscious they kicked seven shades of shit out of him leaving him bruised and battered on the seclusion room floor. He was transferred to a high security hospital that night and began what would be a thirty year stay there.

Dean was diagnosed as a violent psychopath, and they threw the key away. He was seen by a new doctor, a thin man with a poker-face, also with glasses, who would not give Dean any medication, and had the same conversation with Dean for the next ten years, before he gave up on Dean and left him to his life in Ashworth Hospital.

Dean's family, which consisted of his mother and brother, gave up on him, after a few years of making the trip to see him in Liverpool at Christmas, and Dean was left alone. He gave up taking drugs, took every educational qualification going and every job in the hospital. After thirty years Dean was moved to a medium-security unit in Salford, and then to a flat near Salford shopping City.

On the Bright Side

Dean saw his Social Worker once a month, and apart from that he didn't see anybody, apart from the Asian shopkeeper down the road and the staff at the local Allen's chicken bar. He had put on weight, and felt a lot older than he was. He drank a few cans of lager every night to help him sleep and was a shambling wreck compared to the man who had stabbed Dr Moore with a screwdriver all those years ago.

When his social worker came to see him they had the same conversation as they had always done. Dean asked the social worker why she wouldn't leave him alone and why she was concerned about his drinking. He repeated that his treatment had been a total waste of time for everybody and that although he regretted what had happened to Dr Moore, it was unavoidable and inevitable. His social worker left him that day and said she would never see him again. Dean died a couple of weeks later, asleep in his chair. The police were eventually alerted to the fact he was dead after the local scally's left the door of his flat open. They had taken everything Dean had worth having. There were no suspicious circumstances, just a rotten corpse in a room full of flies that had been there for two months.

www.ingramcontent.com/pod-product-compliance
Ingram Content Group UK Ltd.
Pitfield, Milton Keynes, MK11 3LW, UK
UKHW041413180426
11947UKWH00007B/105